three

three

The Ultimate Student's Guide to Acing
Your Extended Essay and Theory of
Knowledge

ALEXANDER ZOUEV

ZOUEV PUBLISHING

Published 2009
Printed by Lightning Source

ISBN 978-0-9560873-0-0, paperback.

Dedicated to Mom, Dad and Romka– thank you guys for all the loving support and belief.

Special thanks to Ken, Lynn, and Dennis. This book would not be complete if it wasn't for you guys.

TABLE OF CONTENTS

INTRODUCTION

Congratulations on obtaining the easiest, cheapest and most efficient manual on how to maximize your chance of getting all three additional points that the IB has to offer. This guide will ultimately teach you the secrets behind obtaining an "excellent grade" in both the Theory of Knowledge (TOK) and Extended Essay (EE) components of the IB. Whether you are reading this to simply get a passing grade, aiming to get one or two bonus points, or even if you are ambitious and want to acquire that impressive A in both components – this manual is for you.

The requirements of the IB Diploma Program include following a TOK course and writing an EE of up to 4,000 words. At the core of the 'IB hexagon' you will be able to find these two requirements, along with CAS. The IBO describes the EE as 'a substantial piece of writing' that 'enables students to investigate a topic of special interest that they have chosen themselves'. TOK is described as a course that 'encourages students to think about the nature of knowledge' and 'make connections across the academic areas.' As a result, it is understandable why both have been noted to be great in helping students make the transition from school to university – a preparation for higher education. These two components are marked on a scale from A to E and are combined to form a joint total of zero to three points (see the matrix provided by the IB if you haven't already). These points are then added onto your final IB Diploma score. As you can see on the matrix, it is relatively difficult to obtain all three additional points. Even having "average" C grades in both components will only give you one point.

So before you dive into the mysterious world of IB additional points you may want to ask yourself: "Who am I to listen to some stranger's advice on what to do for my TOK and EE?" Well, you are absolutely correct to question me. After all, I have never taught the TOK class or done an EE course, nor am I in any way affiliated with the IB and I do not have a teaching degree of any sort. However, there's absolutely no need to panic. As you will discover over the next pages, my firsthand experience in the IB diploma has taught me all the tricks and tips on how to maximize your marks with minimal effort.

Having completed my IB diploma in 2007 with an overall score of 43 and obtaining all three bonus points, I may have more answers and insight than others currently working in the field. I know exactly how it feels to be an average student struggling with the program, looking for all the correct resources and answers with minimal effort and time-wasting. What I can offer you is fool-proof advice and techniques on how to get As in both your TOK and EE without having to work your butt off too much.

So, what can you expect from this short but sweet manual to success in TOK and the EE? Well, if you follow this correctly and put in some effort and determination, you can, I firmly believe, obtain a grade A in both. If, however, you are someone less ambitious and are just struggling to get the grade in one of the components, then just flip to the relevant section. And, finally, if you are someone who is predicted to fail your EE and doesn't have a clue about how to pass TOK, then this book is definitely for you.

No matter how little natural academic ability you have, I firmly believe that, with minimal effort on your part, you surely must get some bonus points if you read this manual correctly. There is no absolutely effortless way to get good grades in TOK and EE; there are, however, ways that will save you energy, time, and effort – but ultimately give you a much higher grade than expected.

For those of you reading to find any tips on plagiarism, cheating or any unethical method to get all three bonus points - you are out of luck.

My tips and techniques are 100% in line with the rules and regulations of the IB. Nonetheless, there will undoubtedly be critics and academics who suggest that a lot of what I recommend is somewhat unethical and not in line with what the IB program is supposed to teach students. I find this idea ridiculous because there are countless students getting high grades in the EE/TOK and succeeding without actually working their socks off and becoming perfect IB students. What you need to understand is that there is "cheating" and then there is "tactical and efficient study techniques", and there is a thick line separating the two concepts. What this book will ultimately teach you to do is become masters of manipulating the resources at your disposal efficiently and tactically, without having to resort to any unethical practices.

The IB "bonus point" system is a gift to you. They are basically asking you whether you want three more points to be added to your final total. Why would you say no? I have seen some of the smartest and hardest-working students fail to achieve all three. In fact, many teachers will tell you that very few actually get all three bonus points (statistics provided by the IBO show that only 8.69% achieved all three bonus points in May 2006 and 8.12% in May 2007). Why this is so simply amazes me.

All you need to do is get one A and one B in either your EE or TOK. So, if you aim for A's in both, then surely you will get an A in at least one of them, right? Well, I only wish it was that easy. The bad news is that you need to work extremely hard to achieve a grade A in either of the two components. The good news is that anyone, of any academic ability, no matter how clever, can achieve the three points. You need to get your priorities straight – if you know that you can afford to miss out on those three points because all you need is a pass and you're predicted about 35, then focus on getting a point, maybe two. However, if you are barely passing, and are in desperate need to squeeze some points out anywhere you can find – the "additional points" are the perfect place to start.

You need to get it through your head that these are not *bonus* points. No matter what you call it – bonus, additional, core, or extra points – your final score isn't given out of 42, it's out of 45. In fact, in recent years the IB has made an effort to remind students that the Diploma is a complete package and the points are part of the total score. Therefore you need to do all that you can to make sure you get all three.

On a final note: before you begin reading the ultimate TOK and EE survival guide you will have to pardon my grammar, spelling and probably my language for large parts of the book. I am, after all, your typical university student, so the language I speak is more similar to yours than that of your teacher (which is probably a good thing for you!). Nonetheless, do not be surprised to find mistakes here and there and as much as I will try to keep this properly organized and well-structured, you'll have to excuse me if I sometimes jump from one point to another. Also, as hard as I will try to be a good role model, you will not find a references section or any bibliography (which in IB terms means suicide for your assignment). The reason for this is simple: most of the things I say are pretty much from my own experience and not from any source.

EXTENDED ESSAY

Those two dreaded words. Extended Essay. The EE. Satan's Essay. Whatever you want to call it, there's no denying that amongst all the responsibilities that the IB student is expected to juggle, the compulsory EE is by far the most feared and hated. This 3,500 to 4,000 word mandatory research paper raises many eyebrows when first introduced to IB students. This is usually followed by a tiny voice in your head telling you "4,000 words on ANYTHING over two years? That's easy!" Well, you would think so, wouldn't you? Why, then, do so many IB students find themselves in the beginning of their final year without a draft, without an outline, without even a title idea.

Let's do some simple mathematics. Let's say, hypothetically, that you are given exactly a one-year deadline to finish your EE (it's around that). That's 365 days. Now let's say you are an overachiever and want to write 4,000 words (the upper limit of essay length). According to my calculations, that's 4,000 divided by 365 or around 10.95 words per day. That's it. If you write 10.95 words per day for a year, then you will have completed your extended essay. I hope most of you can manage eleven words a day.

Now, don't be fooled – I'm not suggesting you spread your EE writing exactly over a one year period – I am merely trying to show you how little 4,000 words over a year really is. As part of Economics and Management degree at Oxford, I am required to write a 3000 – 4000 word essay per week. Yup, that's right, an EE per week, and after having done it for the first few weeks, it became easier and easier up until the point where 4,000 words seemed like nothing. The IB, in an attempt to prepare you for this, generously gives you well over a year to write your "masterpiece."

What your aims are will largely depend on what you want to achieve with your EE. Considering you are actually reading this book in full, I will assume you are serious about getting that A grade that you need to get all three of your bonus points and push you closer to that magic 45. Well, then this book will not disappoint you. If, on the other hand, you are someone who just needs to pass the IB diploma with the minimum requirements (which involves passing the EE), you have also come to the right place.

So what is the problem then? Why do so many students struggle to write what seems to be a simple "extended" essay in such a great amount of time? Well, there are a few traps along the way, and hopefully the following guide over the next few pages will teach you how to avoid those traps and have your EE ready in no time.

What Subject?

Now, although there are no real restrictions on the nature of your essay, it must fall within a subject the IB has on offer (published by the IB in the *Vade Mecum*). Please don't be a wise-guy and try to write an essay on a subject that you do not take. Yes, it is actually allowed and I have seen it happen, at times with mediocre success, but usually with utter failure. A typical example: you are obsessed with WWI history, but your school does not teach history at all, yet you insist that your external reading you do in your own time will give you a great idea and basis for an essay. You spew out 4,000 words of something you believe is truly brilliant and hand it in to your middle school history teacher to mark. He thinks it's great, too. You then send it to the IB only to find out you completely missed the History EE guidelines and end up getting a generous grade D.

Another, more common, example is someone who is really passionate about religion and wants to do a paper in world religion. You will most likely end up being incredibly biased and perhaps say very controversial things. I'll probably regret saying this, but the EE and the IB don't deal directly with religion (unless it's the simple appreciation and acceptance of others' beliefs). Some schools have simply begun to ban their students from writing outside of their own subject areas (probably because of the lack of supervisors available). Look, you do six subjects so is it really that difficult to find something that interests you ever-so-slightly within those six?

Make sure you take a look at the detailed package of documents that the IB offers for the Extended Essay, which will include information on what you should expect in writing each essay. I'm not going to outline what the IB documents say because 1) I don't want to source things you can look up yourself and 2) you can look it up yourself! Once you have chosen your subject, you should print out the relevant guide and read it carefully. Also make sure that you have a supervisor available to oversee your EE in that subject area.

So, which Group should you be looking at then? Well, as my personal advice, I would tell you to stay away from any English or language essays unless you truly have a passion for literature and have been published or somehow rewarded for truly excelling in your writing. The reason is quite simple: writing an excellent literature essay is incredibly difficult because it's simply too competitive and many students who believe they are excellent writers and have been told so by numerous teachers are, in fact, quiet average when compared to kids outside of their school. Do not become one of those students who say, "Hah! I'll just take one of my grade A English papers I wrote on *Doll's House* from last year, add 2000 more words and - viola! Extended Essay complete!" It does not work like that. The EE isn't really an extended essay – you can't simply elongate your normal run-of-the-mill English analysis of a literary work and expect to do well. The problem with Group 1 essays is that many will fail to reveal much personal judgement and overuse historical and biographical information. A very subtle balance is required, and this is often very difficult to maintain. EE reports show that students use secondary sources in place of personal opinions and vocabulary is often a problem, along with structure and quotations. The EE is supposed to be a piece of research, which is why I would suggest you stay away from literature because there is little research to be done.

Group 3 topics seem to make very popular EEs – and perhaps with good reason, too. There are virtually no limitations on what you can write about in Geography, Economics, Business Management, History, and so on. If you take a Group 3 topic that you are truly interested in, see if there is anything you have always pondered over but never really researched in depth. Talk to your teachers and coordinators about the success rates in these topics. For subjects like Economics and Business

Management there is always great demand; however, success is varied. I remember an Economics teacher of mine told me that although it is easy to get a B or C in an Economics EE, you have to come up with pretty good material get an A. Please, don't fall into the trap of "Oh, my dad has his own company, so what better way to do research in business/economics than to write an essay about his company!" Just because you have access to thousands of documents for a firm of a friend or a relative does not mean this will help you write an excellent essay in Economics or BM.

A common trouble area with Economics essays is that there is little personal research and not enough analysis of economic theory. Also, as you would with your Economics coursework, don't forget to define all the key economic terms (either on the spot or as an index). At all cost avoid subjective "What if.." questions because this just does not fit well with the EE's Assessment Criteria. And please, for your own good, make sure to narrow the topic down to a sort of small case study.

With regards to History essays, the problem is as you would expect: reliability of secondary sources (probably would be a good idea NOT to use too many websites). Don't forget that your bibliography for a History essay will probably be twice as long as the bibliography in any other subject – so get ready to do some serious citing. Avoid the traditional "arguments for" followed by "arguments against" approach and then a conclusion consisting of "both sides of the argument are equally valid." Yes, it would be worse to produce a one-sided argument, but avoid being too neutral as well.

What about Group 4 then, the sciences? It seems at first that the task would to be akin to a middle school science fair project or simply a longer-than-usual lab report. Don't get your hopes up. Writing an EE in a science is very demanding, as it not only requires you to have the literary ability found in any other EE, but you also must be able to master the process of conducting experiments, taking data, and providing top-of-the line analysis. My personal advice: if you are an excellent laboratory scientist with plenty of experience writing up lab reports and doing numerous research projects and you have an idea for an EE topic that is not discussed in much detail in the syllabus, then go for it. Perhaps more so than with any other group, writing an EE in Group 4 requires that you have a clear idea what you want to research. You need to know exactly what you are doing and have a pretty good idea of what will happen. Sounds a bit demanding, but there's no point in looking at "the effect of sunlight on erection length" if there's clearly no relationship between the two variables! You would be wasting your time starting to write an EE about a scientific relationship that you doubt actually exists. The flipside, however, is that you would be wasting your time doing an experiment for which the outcome is already well documented in standard textbooks. Hence, you face a dilemma.

Moreover, it is very difficult to write an essay that is distinctly a chemistry essay, not shifting over too much to biology or physics. You could end up with an essay that relates very little to your specific science subject. Again, official IB EE reports state that many science essays lack a satisfactory degree of personal input – perhaps using sophisticated lab equipment limits how much personal input one can have. You also face the risk of reaching a somewhat too general conclusion, and analysis of sources and methods used is often too weak because of the high level of sophistication.

Ah, an EE in Group 5: mathematics, computer sciences, perhaps the most overlooked EE subject area. As I have relatively little knowledge about computer sciences, I will primarily be concerned with an EE in mathematics, so any computer science students can look away now. Also, unless you are taking HL Mathematics, you can forget about writing an EE in maths as well. Now, if you are a HL Mathematics student who is not struggling too much with the material and actually enjoys mathematics, then follow my advice and do an EE in it! Trust me, it will probably be the best decision you will make in your IB experience. Yes, it seems a daunting task – how can one write 4000 words on a subject that is primarily concerned with numbers? But once you do a little research, read several past mathematics essays and convince yourself that writing an EE in maths will be no more or less challenging than any other subject, you should begin to worry less about the whole concept. You will not be expected to make a contribution to the knowledge in the mathematical world. Don't worry, they won't expect you to find the next largest prime number or solve Fermat's Theorem.

There is an unbelievable amount of resources available for anyone interested in doing an EE in mathematics. It really does shock me how few students give it a go, let alone think about doing it. In my year, it was me and only one other student that attempted the EE in mathematics (in our school). It was perhaps the most enjoyable and, at the same time, most demanding piece of work I had to do for the IB – but at the end of the day, it was something I could honestly pick up and be proud of. You don't need a Bachelor's degree in mathematics to be able to write an essay in maths. It might well be more demanding than an EE in other subject areas, but your willingness to challenge yourself will not go unrecognized by the EE examiners. Keep in mind that the minimum word limit is altered for EE in mathematics to around 2500 words (which is nothing really) but you do need a significant amount of actual maths in the text as well (which could be a problem).

What about Group 6? Well, I don't know many who have done an EE in visual arts, theatre arts or music, but if you feel you've got a mini art-critic living inside you, then give it a thought. If you plan on pursuing a university degree involved in the arts, then this may well be an opportunity to see what it would be like doing detailed research and analysis in that area. Remember that there is a great element of creativity involved, so if you're finding your Group 6 classes and assignments uninteresting, then perhaps it would be a good idea to stay away from an EE in that area. Don't think that for your art EE you can just analyze the history of graffiti or that for your music essay you can write 50 Cent's biography – it has to be of a quality expected in the IB program.

The bottom line is that you need to take a long and hard look at your HL classes and decide which subject will suit your essay needs best. I know that the emphasis on EE and subjects differs from school to school, so if you are at a school that is really science-intensive and lacking on the mathematics, then it would probably be better to follow that route. You should ensure that you write your EE at HL, not at SL – simply because you will have not learnt the subject in enough detail. If you are doing HL Mathematics, I once again strongly suggest that you at least consider writing an EE in this subject. If not, my next best bet for you would be to look at your Group 3 subjects and choose something from there. If you're more of a scientist than a social scientist, then by all means go for the Group 4; however, be warned of the obstacles and traps that you may have to overcome. Unless you are a truly naturally gifted literary critic and have extraordinary analysis skills, I would strongly advise to stay away from Groups 1 and 2. Similarly, unless you are obsessed with your Group 6 subject, I would not recommend doing an EE in the arts.

Topic Choice

Once you have done the easy part of choosing under which subject your EE will fall, you must begin thinking of a topic or a range of topics that you could write about. Pick something that actually interests you and is motivating. Don't get too excited if you can find a truckload of information online about your topic of interest – that's usually a bad sign. Pick a topic that has barely any research already done on it and is unique in its nature. Remember, however, that this is a research topic and not your ordinary book review – you must have a question, which you can argue and answer.

Also remember that it needs to be very specific – you don't want a topic that is too general. Please, understand just how important your topic choice really is – it will make or break your essay. Choose something that is silly and unprofessional and you will suffer incredibly. Before you decide on a topic, have a talk to your friends about it, Google it, see if there's an appropriate approach that you can take. A paper on "Economic Monopolies" is far too general, but a paper on a specific type of company monopoly, analysed at a more in-depth level, is more appropriate. It is critical to have a focused research question – talk to your supervisor and see if you can narrow your topic even further. A good topic is one that asks something worth asking and that is answerable within 4000 words. Remember also that your topic should not be something that is taught in relatively good depth already in the syllabus (for example, if you are doing a specific English book in your A1 class, you cannot use the same book for your EE).

This is your perfect opportunity to research that little thing that you have always wondered about but that seemed too complicated to ask. Whether it be specific casino techniques to win at blackjack (mathematics) or Hitler's secret homoerotic sex life (history), find something that has great depth and actually interests you. Don't become one of those students who pick a topic that "sounds good" but has no real meaning – you will end up regretting it. If you pick a topic that actually interests you, then there is a greater chance that you will actually work on it! 4,000 words may be difficult if you are summarizing the Bible, but 4,000 words on your favourite television program seems a lot less demanding (DO NOT write about that). You may want to write outlines for several plausible topics, and then see which one would work best.

Another hidden piece of advice about choosing an EE topic is to choose something that is relatively unknown. If your examiner has no clue as to what your topic is about, then you will be able to educate him/her; how much can the examiner criticize you if he/she knows nothing about it him/herself? And, as I said before, if you choose a topic for which you think you will find almost no information, you are in a much better situation than someone who has a multitude of sources from the go.

So how do you go about finding a final topic? Well, it will depend from subject to subject, but usually you will need something to inspire you. For this very reason, you need to start flipping through books concerned with the ideas you plan to write about. For example, if doing an EE in maths, I strongly recommend as a good starting point to look at a book about "100 greatest unsolved mathematical problems" and see if there is something there that interests you. Don't stress out yet! Just because it has not been solved doesn't mean that you will have to solve it! It just means that you can do a good research paper on it – find out what others have been writing and develop your own method at solving the problem. Try contacting some university-level professors and see what they have to say (this doesn't only apply to math, but also to history, economics, the sciences and so on).

The title of your essay (your topic question) does not necessarily have to be in question form. Nonetheless, the title is of incredible importance (see Assessment Criteria). You need to make sure it's precise, concise and clearly shows the focus of the essay. The sooner you get this done, the better – it will drive your essay in the right direction. Remember that the exact wording of your research question is not set in stone; you will be able to go back and modify it later on.

Time Management

Some schools suggest that you spend about 35 - 40 hours on your EE, the IBO suggests approximately 40 hours as well, other schools encourage 80 to 100 hours. No matter where you stand, you can see that a great deal of time will be spent on your essay, which is why you need to manage your time well. I was once amongst those who didn't understand why we had to follow a timeline for our EE and couldn't just do things in our own time. Well, I hate to admit it, but the timeline that the IB sets out ensures that you don't mess up and fall behind. This way, if there are any problems with you essay, they can be detected in the early stages, so that you don't waste your time writing an entire EE only to have it rejected.

Do yourself a favour and ignore any stories you hear from seniors who tell you how they wrote their EE in one sitting, a few days before it was due and got an A for it. Unless you have some magic ability to work productively non-stop for a good 80 hours or so, you will not be able to complete your EE in one sitting – or even in a few sittings. Take my word for it, taking small steps, one at a time, is the key to success. There are limits to this as well, however, so don't fool yourself into thinking that by adding a sentence or two to your essay you have done enough work for the week.

Your IB coordinator should ensure that you more or less follow the deadlines. Make sure you know all the important dates and keep them in your agenda (if you have one) or print them out and post them on your board. There will be dates for having your topic ready, finding your supervisor, getting your outline and bibliography ready and so on. Remember that if you risk falling behind on one of the dates, it could have a domino effect and some serious repercussions.

You will be writing your EE primarily outside of the classroom on your own time and, unlike with school homework, it is unlikely that there will be any check-ups to verify that you are doing the work. It is 'strongly recommended', but not 'required' that your school sets internal deadlines for the stages of completing your EE. Take some responsibility. I know that the workload in your other subjects will be heavy, but don't forget about your EE. I highly recommend finishing the bulk of it over the winter holidays. Also, I wouldn't rely too much on the dates that the coordinator "suggests" you follow – the more ambitious and independent of you should make your own agenda and stick to it. Set yourself specific goals, and if you fall behind, then make sure to catch up at the cost of perhaps even missing some schoolwork or failing a few tests (EE points are a lot more important than your everyday school work). Also, contrary to popular belief, working on your EE over the weekend is not a crime.

Supervision

Before you start writing your EE you will need to have a member of faculty "supervise" your EE so that there is someone to make sure you follow IB guidelines. Be quick and reserve your supervisor first because usually the more popular teachers are filled up with requests within a week – especially for the social science topics such as IB History and IB Economics. I strongly advise getting your subject teacher to be your supervisor because 1) they should know most of the material that the subject encompasses inside out and 2) they will be familiar with the IB program and will know what to expect. For your own good, try not to get a supervisor who does not teach the IB or who is unfamiliar with the demands of the program.

The role of the supervisor is very clear. They are strongly recommended to spend between 3 and 5 hours with you working on your EE. They are not there to write your essay for you, and you shouldn't protest against them for not helping you enough. There is a set of guidelines that supervisors must follow (once again, see IB documentation) in order to ensure that each student in every school gets an equal chance to maintain fairness. They are mainly there for support and encouragement, along with making sure that you keep up with the deadlines and don't plagiarize. They will also need to give you advice and guidance on undertaking research. The words "encouragement, support and reassurance" do not mean that they will write sentences for you. They will also decide on a set amount of time that they can devote to your EE (which is a good reason to choose a supervisor who doesn't have his/her hands full all the time).

Your supervisor is your friend. Remember that it is not an obligation for a teacher to supervise an EE – so make sure you don't abuse that privilege. Treat them like trash, and you will get trash in return. Don't be too demanding, but then again, don't let them get away from their promises. Once again, have a good read of what the IB suggests the supervisor does, and if your supervisor isn't up to standards, then you make the case to your coordinator to reach a solution.

I hate to say it, and this might come as an unfortunate shock for most you, but I would say that your EE's success depends about 75% on your input, and 25% on your supervisor's. Although they don't actually write anything that goes into your essay or give you that much advice, the report that they submit to the examining board (which includes his/her personal comments) is incredibly important. Pick a clueless and incoherent supervisor and you will not only pay the price in terms of feedback, but also you risk having all the formalities that are involved with the submission of the EE to be incomplete. This is why I strongly suggest finding a supervisor who is confident with the IB Diploma system and who has at least a year or two of EE experience. I wish I could tell you that no matter how poor your supervisor is, you can still get an A, but due to the increasingly important role they play, this is not the case.

Look, let's be realistic. The more experience the teacher has with the IB and the EE, the more they will be able to offer in terms of what to do and what to best avoid. I know this is a problem in many schools that are just starting the IB program and where almost all the teachers have zero IB experience. But, if you have the opportunity to work with a teacher who has been teaching the subject for more than a few years, then I would strongly suggest you go for that. Trust me, you don't want to end up complaining about your new A-level accredited chemistry teacher just because he has no idea what an EE is in the first place.

Remember that it is your supervisor who has the final say on whether or not your essay will even get a passing grade. So if you choose a supervisor who is clueless about what a pass is, then you risk failing your entire IB diploma if your paper ends up not satisfying the examiners' requirements for a passing grade. Your supervisor should have you rewrite your paper if you are borderline passing (however, if you have been following this guide, this should not be the case!).

Find a teacher who will best match your subject and perhaps give you sources (books, websites, magazines, etc.) that others cannot. They need to be able to provide you with constructive criticism and guidance. Remember that you are not tied down to your supervisor with regards to help and advice. You can consult your seniors and friends for general EE advice. If it is topic specific, then make sure you source the person in your bibliography. At the end of the day though, your supervisor is the one who needs to complete all the formalities that are described in the EE guide.

Getting Started / Research

There are few things in life that compare to looking at a blank page, struggling to come up with an eye-catching introduction. My best advice for you (and advice that is usually given to beginner writers) is simply to put the pen to paper and jot your ideas down. The introduction might not be the best place to start, so start jotting down your research in clear, coherent form, and eventually you will be able to start structuring your essay properly.

Your best bet before putting the pen to paper would be to conduct some serious research. Hopefully, your school will have given you a brief introduction into how to write a research paper, but there are a few things you need to keep in mind while researching. Depending on your topic, it could be that research is either incredibly easy or incredibly hard. The latter is probably the better situation to be in. For my EE, I wrote a paper on a 2,000-year-old mathematical riddle called "Alhazen's Problem." Googling it got me almost nowhere. Yes, I found some news articles here and there and some definitions and outlines, but in terms of raw research done, there was almost nothing. I didn't worry too much, because the internet (as great as it is) doesn't hold the answer to everything.

As an IB student, you need to learn to become very enquiring about what you are learning. There are several search engines designed specifically for research papers that you might need to consult (JSTOR, SSRN and Proquest to name a few). Yes, some are free, but some have a subscription fee. You need to figure out what it is you really want. Alternatively, you can try popping down to your local city library (because you've already gone to your school library, right?) and see if they have anything of interest. Be creative with your research. I remember having to email an Oxford professor to see if he could provide me with any information (unfortunately he totally ignored me!). Don't give up though, and keep in mind that all the other students are doing exactly what you should try and avoid. As great as Wikipedia, Bized and Dictionary.com are, you will not stand out amongst the crowd if your research does not go beyond that.

Whilst on the subject of research, make sure you take a look at as many EEs you can get your hands on in your subject area (preferably good ones). I don't mean read them through beginning to end, I'm just saying you may get some ideas about where to start once you see what a good EE is supposed to look like. The IB have now launched a collection of 50 great EE's (all of which were awarded a grade A) available in CD/DVD format for about a hundred dollars. Hopefully your school will buy a copy of this to keep in the library. If not, then try to get your hands on it by some other means (perhaps chipping in a fiver with twenty or so friends). It's not essential you look at many past EE's, but I would highly recommend it. By reading previous essays, you can identify common pitfalls as well as strengths in various topics.

Structure

For most of you this will be the first time that you write an essay that has clear sections and a clearly defined structure. You should aim to provide a personal exploration of the topic and try your best to argue your points in a professional manner. Don't jump all over the place with arguments. Make sure at the end that you are able to make a contents page that will outline where you can find all the different sections.

I can't teach you in the space of a few paragraphs how to be able to write with good structure. That is something that comes with experience, good English teachers and a bit of luck. What I can tell you, however, is that unless you have some material to work with, structure will be even harder. If you have 4,000 words worth of material spread over 20 pages, then structuring becomes much less of a problem than if you have 400 words and no idea where you're going.

The main issue of structure will be writing the body of your essay, which should be presented in the form of a reasoned argument. You can choose to have sub-headings if this will help your readers navigate and understand your essay better.

Do yourself a favour and stick to the IB guidelines. Find out exactly what your title page needs to contain, and make sure that you have no more, no less than what is required. The abstract also has very specific requirements that you need to look up, along with the main body, bibliography and conclusion. All of this information can be found right under your nose; the difference between you and the IB candidates who score more than you is that the latter will actually consult the IBO guide and use it to their advantage! Make sure you get all the basics correct, including your name and candidate number in the correct place on every page.

Constantly keep in mind how essential organization and structure of ideas actually is to your essay. You need to be very clear-cut and, please, avoid ambiguity at all costs. Remember that if you have clear sections, then you are already doing some of the work for your examiner in the sense that he/she will not have to waste time finding where your introduction/conclusion is.

Presentation

Make sure your final product is something that you can actually be proud of. No massive WordArt titles and colourful page borders, please. Pretend you are in university and are handing in your Doctorate. Make sure the paper is word-processed, double spaced, 12 point font (if you insist on using Comic Sans, then the IB is probably not for you), margins of standard size, and do not neglect to number the pages accurately. Make it look neat and not like some scribble that you rushed in the last few days. Have some logical presentation. It would probably be a good idea to number all of your graphs, maps and tables so that it's easier to refer to them in your text (only use diagrams and illustrations if they serve a purpose!). Even if what you have written in your EE is spectacular, if it looks like something that a five-year-old child scribbled out, then you have just wasted your time.

Word Count

You will almost definitely have a problem with your word count whilst writing your EE. Just make sure it is a problem of having too many words rather than too little. You're not in middle school anymore. Stop opening up "word count" to see how many words you have until you reach that dreaded 3,500 minimum limit, and then, to top it all off throw in another hundred or so words or lie and say you wrote 3,600 "just so the examiner doesn't think I'm an underachiever." You need to just sit and write and write and write until you feel like you have exhausted your topic. Cutting down will rarely be a problem, because you will have both "good" material and "poor" material on the page. Aim for 4,000, but don't make it *exactly* 4,000. Around 3,900 is ideal, really. For those of you wondering, "Why would I want to write any more than 3,500 if that is the set minimum?" –the short and honest truth is that 3,500 words could imply that the topic was not investigated thoroughly and you struggled to say any more.

Don't mess it up either. Find out and verify what is included in the word count (intro, body, conclusion, questions) and exactly what is not included (abstract, contents page, footnotes, title page). You will be penalized if you go over or under the limit, so save yourself the hassle and make sure you do your counting right. Essays containing more than 4,000 words will be subject to penalties and examiners are not expected to read and assess the material in excess of the limit

Documents

Look, don't be stupid. The IB doesn't publish hundreds of pages of information and guidelines about the EE for no reason. READ IT. Believe me, the majority of students go on trusting their IB coordinator and EE supervisor alone, not even for a second thinking that it would probably be a good idea to read the EE instructions for themselves. Don't become one of these students. Get online, find all the relevant PDFs issued by the IBO that concern the EE and it would probably be a good idea to print them out as well. Highlight the relevant parts that you would probably not have noticed and consult the guidelines every once in a while.

You need to go to your IB coordinator and ask to see all relevant material provided by the IB with regards to the Extended Essay. It is a requirement for your school to ensure that your EE conforms to the regulations published in the official IB EE guide.

Assessment Criteria

Ok, read this very carefully: the grading criteria that the IB provides for your EE is undoubtedly the most important resource that you will use in completing your EE. The vast majority of students don't even know that such grading criteria exist. Don't be counted among them! Remember, although the method of assessment judges each student in relation to the criteria and not in relation to the work of other students, you are still in a way competing against the rest of the students writing an EE in your area, so you want to make sure you do positive things that they will probably forget to do. The most important of these is making sure your EE ticks all the boxes in the grading criteria, flawlessly.

The EE will be graded by examiners appointed by the IBO using a scale of a maximum of 36 points. This maximum score is made up of the total criterion levels available for each essay. Your EE will be scrutinized and the examiner will literally read each criterion, starting with level 0, until a level is reached that best describes the work being assessed.

As of the new EE regulations that came into place starting 2009, there is no distinction between 'general marks' and 'subject specific marks'. Now there is only the generic 'Assessment Criteria', however examiners are still suggested to consult further advice on interpreting the assessment criteria within the guidelines of each subject in the 'Details – subject specific' section of the IB published guide on the EE.

Now I'm not exaggerating. Once you think you have come somewhere near the completion of your EE, sit down, EE in one hand, Assessment Criteria in the other. Start with the first descriptor and go through each section. Give yourself what you honestly think you deserve in each part. Now the IB is very picky about their assessment of EEs. They will have someone sit down with your essay and do exactly as you are doing. Here's another fact you probably didn't know: they are paid by the paper. What this means is that they will want to get through each paper as fast as they can – use this to your benefit and make your essay more accessible for the examiner to mark.

This means paying extra close attention to the exact wording in the assessment criteria. If it says "the approach used to answer the research question..." then you better make sure you have the words "research question" somewhere in the beginning of your essay, and when you begin to answer it, make sure you say "the approach I will be using to answer my research question is..." I know, it sounds ridiculous, but believe me, you will gain points for small things like that. If they ask for an abstract that "states clearly the research question that was investigated, how the investigation was undertaken and the conclusion of the essay," then you damn well make sure it does! In fact, the abstract is probably the easiest section to score full marks on. If you read the guidelines, you literally cannot go wrong.

Get this into your head right now: the IB is not going to read your EE and give you a grade depending on how "good" your essay is. Even if you write a world-changing piece on a mathematical breakthrough, you must tick all the appropriate boxes in the Assessment Criteria. Similarly, if you write a pretty crap essay in your subject but manage to fulfil most of the requirements in the Assessment Criteria, then you will be surprised at how many marks you can get for simply following the guidelines.

The highest descriptors are not reserved for flawless essays, and if you deserve the highest mark then you will obtain it. There is no arithmetic relationship between the descriptor numbers – a level 4 is not necessarily twice as good as a level 2 performance. Moreover, it is also important to understand that scoring high in one criterion will not necessarily mean you will receive similar marks in the other descriptors.

Here is a great tip I learned from my own EE coordinator to make sure you get full marks in stating your topic question. Look carefully at the grading criterion part A, the research question. If you want full marks you need to make sure "the research question is clearly stated in the introduction and is sharply focused, making effective treatment possible within the word limit." Although I can't ensure that you fulfil the second part of that statement, with regards to the first part I have a great piece of advice for you. If you want your research question to stand out, why not make sure that in your introduction, you place your research question in a clearly bordered rectangular box, perhaps even shaded lightly. Use a bold font and place your question in quotations (see my EE if you still don't know what I mean). This could easily get you a mark or two (which might not seem like a lot out of 36), but you need to understand that if you work in a similar manner throughout the whole Assessment Criteria – probing every sentence and word that the IB use - you can easily pick up a few points here and there for just minor adjustments.

Although there is no longer a 'subject specific' grading criterion, you should not ignore the idea that your EE is specific to your subject.

The IB still publishes subject specific 'details' which examiners will read before marking your essay. Have a good look at these documents because often there will be examiner reports and comments on common pitfalls and highlights of essays written in your subject.

If something is lacking in clarity or if you don't think you have met the requirements, then go back and make changes. Keep doing this until you believe you can get at least 90% on your EE – chances are you will be getting an A or a B. Be realistic when you are doing this and get it into your head: the Assessment Criteria is the most important factor in deciding how successful your EE will be!

As I briefly mentioned before, try and make life easier for your examiner. You don't want to waste his/her time if he/she can't tell where your introduction finishes and your essay body begins. Similarly, if your conclusion is muddled together with your evaluation (if you have one), then it becomes more difficult to grade. Although not obligatory, I would strongly recommend having sections (chapters) in your essay – that way you can expand your contents page to be more detailed.

The most successful essays written every year are done by students who have kept the Assessment Criteria as a poster up on their bedroom wall. If you know what the examiner wants, you can provide it for him/her. They will be able to skim through it and give you a good mark if you tick all the boxes that they want ticked. Bottom line (and I'm sorry for repeating myself, but this is crucial to your success): treat the Assessment Criteria as the key to getting your A-grade essay.

Sourcing

As the EE is a research paper, you would be foolish to leave your bibliography blank. In fact (and many teachers would probably disagree with me) you should ensure that you have a very wide range of sources and a lot of them. When the examiners look at your bibliography and see that you have consulted the good ol' Wikipedia here and there, Googled this and that, and stuck in a few sentences from your school textbook, they will not be impressed.

On the other hand, if you have magazine articles, dictionaries, real person interviews, university level texts, and newspaper articles in your bibliography, you're in a whole different league. Yes, it varies in difficulty from subject to subject, and depending on the topic, you might struggle to find even ten sources of information. That being said, don't be a parrot either and simply source everyone and everything you read. Collecting material that is not actually relevant to your research question is not recommended, as well as citing sources that are not actually used.

The other benefit from using book and paper sources is that they are reliable sources. By using the internet to do most of your research you risk quoting biased and sketchy information – be sceptical and read with a critical mind (like an IB student should!). Use your brain.

Also, you must ensure that your bibliography and method of sourcing is 100% in line with what the IB expects. There are a billion websites on the internet that will do the bibliography for you; some might even give you the footnotes/endnotes – just make sure you get this correct. You can use whichever system you prefer – whether it be an in-text system or a number system with footnotes – as long as you remain consistent. Just remember: you have to give credit if you are using someone else's work!

My own IB coordinator gave me an invaluable piece of advice when it comes to citing sources: when you find a useful source, drop everything you are doing and write down all the publication information (which you need for the bibliography) immediately on a set of note-cards. I thought it was a bit silly at first, but do this crucial step and you will thank me later on. When the time comes for you to actually formally write up your bibliography, you will have everything you need at your fingertips.

Another good reason to have proper citations is to eradicate any suspicion of plagiarism. Whilst small shortcomings in your referencing may cost you a mark or two, major problems could spell trouble for you in terms of plagiarism. Note any changes that have been recently made to the bibliography methods for the new EE's – notably that bibliographies now only have to list the sources you have cited and not the sources you have consulted.

Plagiarism

Simple. Don't do it. Yea ok, it's unethical, it's unfair, it's bad – all of that is true. More importantly, however, you will get caught. I have seen it all: plain copy and pasting off the Internet, the purchasing of essays for ridiculous amounts of money, and even getting specialist friends of your parents to write your paper for you. Even if the anti-plagiarism computer software (which has advanced incredibly over recent years) fails to catch you, it's your tutor's job to decide if the work is yours or not. Turn-it-in.com has been somewhat of a breakthrough in the way research papers are monitored these days. Keep in mind you will have to submit an electronic version of your EE – so spare yourself the drama and make sure you don't copy and paste.

I always say that the only person dumber than someone who knowingly plagiarises is the person who does it unknowingly. Fail to include a proper bibliography and cite certain sources "by accident" and you will taste the same consequences as the kid who did it on purpose. Don't make that mistake.

Now look, if you have been writing poorly written essays for as long as you can remember, and then all of a sudden you hand in a Doctorate-worthy masterpiece, flawlessly written and organized to perfection – your tutor (unless he's like you) will notice the sudden change in writing style and will question you extensively. Nothing looks worse than a student unable to answer simple questions about a paper he/she supposedly wrote. Reward is just not worth the risk, considering you are capable of producing something of a greater quality.

Come on now, it's only 4,000 words! Are you really telling me you are not able to write 4,000 words yourself without cheating and plagiarising? If that's the case, then good luck with university or whatever career you choose to pursue after high school.

Finished?

My teacher once said that your EE will never really be a finished product – there will simply come a time when you must hand it in. Keep this in mind whilst proofreading your essay and more importantly writing your conclusion. Please, under no circumstances write as your final sentence "In conclusion, there are .... The End" – the IB does not expect you to know every single detail about your topic and give a concrete and flawless answer. If you still have unanswered questions relating to the topic, then make sure you say so (and, if possible, suggest how you would, given more resources and time, go about answering these questions).

Now you think you're done? Well think again. Go back constantly and make sure you have done everything as best as you can. They are handing you an opportunity to get an A. This is not an exam for which you need to study; it is a piece of work that you can take as many hours as you need to complete. Go online and find an EE checklist, make sure you hit all the nails on the head before you hand in anything.

If you're still convinced that you have completed your final draft, then I suggest you hold up your EE and ask yourself the following: is it something that I am proud of? Are you not embarrassed to read it? Is this your best work? If you can answer "yes" to the last question then you're probably ready to submit.

The Viva Voce

In the new format of the Extended Essay, the IBO recommends supervisors and schools to conclude the EE process with a short interview, called the Viva Voce. It is a recommended conclusion to the extended essay process.

The point of the viva voce is to eradicate any suspicions of plagiarism as well as provide an opportunity to reflect on what has been learned from the experience. The whole interview will last 10 to 15 minutes and you should be ready to answer any questions your supervisor may have about your essay, including questions on specific sentences, citations, references but also on why you chose the topic, your high and low points of the process, and what interested you the most.

It may be possible that you won't have this interview, as it is not obligatory per se. Nonetheless, I would recommend you prepare yourself to answer questions about your methods, choice of topic, conclusion, and skills you learnt during the process. Remember however that you will not be graded on this interview as there is no grading criterion for it and it's not compulsory.

To be honest, this interview should not pose any threat to the success of your EE. It is really just used as a way to catch students who are suspected of plagiarism off guard. Unless you have serious short-term memory loss, you will do fine. The process should end positively and is a nice conclusion to the completion of such a major piece of work.

Additional Resources

When I started the IB program some three years back, there was some material available on the Internet with regards to help with the EE. Now, having a quick look around, it seems as if there has been an incredible shift in interest and an increase in information with regards to the diploma program. This guide is supposed to help you survive the EE – but by all means, don't let your research end there. Make it your primary goal to gather as much information as you can. Find out what others are writing about the EE, ask your peers, keep Googling "Extended Essay help". No matter how hard I try, there's only so much I can put into this guide. You need to understand that there are hundreds, if not thousands, of good websites, books, and other resources out there that can compliment this guide and your quest for more information. Keep checking the IBO website store to see if there is anything worth purchasing (or begging your school to purchase) with regards to the EE.

Don't exaggerate the difficulty and magnitude of the Extended Essay. Take it seriously, but don't get obsessed with it (if that makes any sense). Just remember what the real aim here is: to get an A or a B in order to boost your chances of getting all three bonus points.

Three points is less than half of what just one of your courses can potentially give you (seven points). That being said, they are probably the easiest three points to obtain as there is no examination involved (so you can work your butt off and guarantee yourself the points). Don't make the EE more overwhelming than it really is.

Remember that if you mess up your EE, then you can wave two years of hard high school struggling bye-bye. It's not optional – it's mandatory. To be quite honest with you, after having completed the EE, I can understand why the IB would want you do write a 4,000-word essay. You won't find the same or any close equivalent in the A-level program or SAT's, and if you go on to university, you will be able to separate the kids who did IB from the non-IB kids almost instantly by their ability to write long, well-structured essays. The EE, if written correctly, will give you a massive advantage later on in your further studies – trust me.

Since the IB suggests that the EE should take around 40 hours to complete, you could, in theory, leave the EE to the last weekend before its due. There's a funny old saying about this extensive deferment of work – "the best way to get something done is to start it today." Start your EE the weekend it is assigned, finish it by end of Christmas break, and have it fully cleaned up and edited by end of Easter break – do that and you can take the rest of the time off laughing as your fellow IB peers continue to fool themselves.

Theory of Knowledge

Boring. Useless. Naptime. "Wannabe philosophy" – just some of the words I have heard students use to address the TOK component of IB. My own opinion is not of importance, but let's just say I have felt very mixed feelings when it comes to Theory of Knowledge. As with many things in the IB Diploma, TOK has its upsides and downsides. The bad news first: it's controversial, at times utterly boring, and you might struggle to accept what the course is trying to teach. The good news: it's less work than the Extended Essay if you want an A grade and there is almost no academic ability involved. Whether you are an A student or an F student it doesn't matter – *anyone* can do reasonably well in TOK.

TOK is the only course taken by every IB diploma and certificate candidate around the world. The implications of this are immense. Your work is being compared to the other 200,000 or so IB kids taking it every year. So why do so many students hate the course? I don't really know where to start – it could be the lack of quality teachers, the "incompleteness" of the syllabus, or the fact that not a single other high school program being taught around the world has anything that even remotely compares to TOK. Moreover, it is frustrating for students how subjective the course can become. It can easily be the case that two teachers in the same school will teach and mark in completely different manners. The classes can become tedious as you start to find yourself questioning things such as your own existence and having endless repetitive debates about "how we know" something. The subject material found in TOK is mostly unfamiliar to both teachers and students, therefore making it all the more difficult to teach.

Out of all my classmates, I probably disagreed with the course more than anyone else (ironically getting the top grade for my essay/presentation). Get this into your head now: no matter how much you hate the course or disagree with it, it should have no impact on your ability to get a top mark. Yes, some will tell you that if you're positive and interested in the material then you will be more successful. This guide, however, will teach you exactly what to do (and what not to do) in order to succeed – regardless of your personal interest in TOK.

One of the reasons I find TOK so controversial is that some teachers insist on teaching TOK as the (ultimate) knowledge course. As if it's accepted worldwide that there are four Ways of Knowing and a concrete seven

Areas of Knowledge. The fact of the matter is, outside your TOK class, no single other non-IB educated person will know what you're talking about. Philosophers have debated for years on knowledge issues and will continue to do so. It might be a sad truth, but the TOK diagram is almost "fictional" in the sense that it's made by the IB, for the IB. I'm not trying to take away the valuable lessons in knowledge that TOK does offer; however, I want you to understand that there is so much more depth and so many more interesting things to learn about knowledge outside the IB course. Just to show you how ambiguous and intangible the course is, in recent syllabuses the "perception" Way of Knowing has been replaced with "sense perception." This shouldn't concern you too much, but just keep in mind that whilst you are trying to ace your essay and presentation, there is much more to philosophy and knowledge than TOK tries to teach.

So what will it take? Well, the TOK component consists of a 1200–1600 word essay and a ten minute presentation. I have to admit that both are probably going to end up being extremely dull, but at least you should be happy about the fact that you will be getting very high marks.

Essay

The externally-moderated essay is worth 40 points (the presentation is worth only 20), which means that it has twice as much bearing on your final TOK grade. This is probably a good thing as it is externally assessed (no matter how much you irritated your TOK teacher throughout the years, he/she can't get revenge on you). You should be aiming realistically to get 30 – 35 points, which is not that easy. I have outlined several tips below that will guide you in the right direction.

The essay will require you to show your TOK assessment skills in a prescribed title that you probably would have never chosen if you could have come up with your own essay title. Examples will play a key role in your essay as well as a TOK-based analysis of those examples.

Question choice

Half of the work in writing a good TOK essay involves choosing a good essay title. Out of the list of ten that the IBO provides, there will be one or two that have potentially more marks up for grabs than the others. Do not make the easy but fatal mistake of saying, "Ah, screw those long questions. The shorter the question the easier it is." I would actually argue the other way around. Shorter questions tend to carry a lot of ambiguity, whereas with longer questions, you know exactly what you are supposed to write about.

Look for questions that have a lot of TOK terminology in them and ones that will give you an opportunity to provide a lot of "interesting" TOK arguments. Remember that the essay will demonstrate your ability to link knowledge issues to Areas of Knowledge and Ways of Knowing. Don't go for the questions that you think are interesting to write about; instead, go for the questions you think your TOK teacher would find interesting to read. Anything that specifically asks you to compare, contrast, explain or describe an Area of Knowledge or Way of Knowing is much better than a question that lacks TOK material. If you don't think that the title suggests problems found in knowledge, then it is best to choose another one.

Take your time when choosing the title. Titles usually come out very early, and you usually don't need to make your final choice until your second year. Think long and hard about which question will allow you to demonstrate your TOK knowledge best and one that will let you critically assess. As a rule of thumb, the more TOK key words in the title, the better. Also, avoid questions that could have ambiguous meanings. Remember that you will be paying close attention to the terminology in the question and that you will be expected to address every aspect of the question.

Make sure you know exactly what you are being asked to do. Questions that require you to "evaluate" and "assess" a certain claim will require you to provide arguments for and against. Don't oversimplify the question and make sure to take into account all possible "grey areas." Furthermore, you need to understand every single word that is part of the question. You may think you know what is being asked, but make sure you look up different interpretations of the word (it's unlikely that you would include this in your writing, but at least you will be more prepared when you start writing).

If you're choosing a question that *kind of* sounds like something you could do a great essay on and you're hoping you can just edit the title just a tiny bit, well, think again. The title must be used exactly as given, without any form of alteration. If you fail to follow these instructions, you risk obtaining a failing or incomplete grade. Work with what you are given and focus on the title at hand.

Last but not least, don't be a sheep. Do not think that by choosing a topic that is more popular you will be able to get some good ideas from your friends doing the same topic. Since the essay is capped at 1600 words, there will be literally pages and pages of material to write about, which you will need to filter. Don't worry about not having good enough examples or arguments. And also, if you were to "borrow" an idea from a friend's essay that would probably be plagiarism anyways.

Where to start

My best advice to those who are just about to start writing their TOK essays would be to get your hands on as much official IB-TOK material as possible and highlight everything that is relevant to your essay. With TOK, you are limited with the information you can find on the Internet because the nature of the course is too specific. You can try Googling "perception as a way of knowing" and you will find two types of information – stuff written specifically for the IB TOK program, and stuff that other philosophers/writers have to say. Only the former is of any use to you. As you will find out later on, these "Areas of Knowledge" and "Ways of Knowing" are by no means world acknowledged. Only in the IB program will you find such specific classifications.

Nonetheless, do a fair amount of research on your topic within the realm of TOK. Hopefully your school has some TOK books lying around in cobwebs and dust – get those out and make notes on your question. This is the best type of resources because they are written by the type of people who will be marking your exam – the true believers of TOK.

Unfortunately, you will have to be pretty good at convincing your examiner that you know what you are talking about. You need to show strong evidence of the Problems of Knowledge, Areas of Knowledge and Ways of Knowing. My best advice for you is to read the official IB TOK books that have been issued over the years. There is a lot of "fun" activities and rubbish in them, but you'd be surprised at how often you will find a quote here or there that will fit into your essay perfectly (of course not plagiarised).

Organization and Structure

My help here is going to be extremely limited. I'm sorry, but nothing I say will really make you write in a more structured manner or teach you how to organize your thoughts – it is something that you must learn and perfect over time. That being said, make sure you keep the essay title with you at all times on a separate piece of paper. Keep glancing at it from time to time and if you ever think a paragraph or sentence is simply too irrelevant, then take it out.

When you start the actual writing process, be sure to type out the question exactly as it is written, word for word, at the top of your paper (including the question number). Throw everything into quotations and in a bold font. This saves the examiner any confusion as to which question you are doing.

Your structure will largely depend on the nature of your question. If it is a simple compare and contrast between two Areas of Knowledge, then you could spend three or four paragraphs explaining how they are similar, and follow that up by the same treatment of how they differ, leaving a few paragraphs at the end for final analysis and conclusion. If you are asked specifically about different Areas of Knowledge, your approach may be to go through each one and explore how it relates to your topic question. Eventually you will end up forming some sort of concluding argument. Keep in mind that there is no single optimal way to write the essay, you need to use your judgement and decide what suits your essay best.

When your paper is complete, you should be able to read it and applaud yourself on your good transitions and structure. Have some rhythm and don't jump paragraph to paragraph talking about completely unrelated matters. If you are still struggling, consult an English book that guides you on how to have smooth transitional paragraphs.

Writing

The actual writing process should take far less time than the research and the post-writing procedures you have to go through. 1200 words is nothing really. As you would with the EE, try to push yourself closer to the 1600 target and further away from the minimum. If you have done your research and thought about the essay enough, writing it should not be an issue. Rarely will a 1200 word paper get a grade A – show the examiner that you are not a minimalist student.

Don't mess around when it comes to essay length. You can try and outsmart the IB by lying about the word count, however, that would be incredibly stupid as an electronic version is included. Remember that the word count includes the main parts of the essay along with any quotations. It does not include acknowledgements or references given in footnote form, or the bibliography. At the end of the essay, you should indicate your word count in bold to signal to your examiner that you followed the guidelines.

Your introduction should capture the reader's attention and summarize what the bulk of your essay will argue. Keep it short but well-written. Avoid any grossly meaningless opening statements and get into it straight away.

Remember that you can't really afford to have a long introduction given the word count limitations, so be sure to establish your topic and provide clarity. Discuss the key concepts and include an insight into the major arguments of your essay. Also, while writing, keep in mind that it is probably best not to expand ideas too far – if you still have words to spare at the end, you can always go back and develop arguments in more depth.

As far as definitions are concerned, be rational. Don't give the Oxford Dictionary definition of "knowledge" – let about 10,000 other kids make this very mistake. You should know better than that. In fact, don't use the dictionary unless it's absolutely vital. When describing concepts such as "knowledge" or "proof," you are better off using the words of various intellectuals, coupled with your own interpretations rather than a wordy dictionary definition. Don't be fooled into thinking that by providing a definition, you have cleared up all ambiguities and complications associated with the concept – that would be stupid.

Some will tell you it's better to write a lot about a little instead of a little about a lot, whilst others will suggest you include as many TOK concepts as possible. The optimal, my experience has shown, is somewhere in between. If there is any specific terminology in the prescribed title then it should be clearly addressed and discussed in the essay. You do need to make sure you tick off an adequate number of Areas of Knowledge and Ways of Knowing, otherwise, the examiner will not know how comfortable you are with the course. At the same time the word limit will not allow you to go through each one by one. Filter out the best material to discuss. Don't sacrifice quality for quantity. If your essay lacks depth of analysis, your examiner will remember this shallowness in treatment when marking your essay. Clarity is the key – think and write clearly.

Some teachers may warn you against using "I" or "me" in an essay of this sort. This becomes very difficult to do when you discuss your personal experiences and your own beliefs. Try to get around this by avoiding amateur statements like "I believe that... I think that..." and replace them with statements like "judging from my personal experience.... Having witnessed something similar myself..." Catch my drift?

The conclusion is probably the best place to present your personal opinion. Here you are allowed to take a stand because you have already gone through all of the arguments and counterarguments in the body of your essay. Again, avoid being too narrow-minded and show an awareness of a variety of opinions.

Also, if you haven't yet convinced your examiner by the time he gets to your conclusion that you have shown personal engagement, then at least you can achieve this in the last paragraph he/she will read.

Always go back and clean up your essay, making sure you have no elementary spelling and grammar mistakes. Although you will not get punished specifically for having any of that, it can potentially interfere with your structure and the "flow" of your essay.

Nothing Controversial

Ok, this is going to be very difficult to write, but it needs to be put out there. The name of the game is: tell them what they want to hear. Look, I know how you feel. It's that feeling of wanting to rip your hair out if you hear another person mention their WoKs or AoKs. Now, you can either be a rebel and fight the entire IB system and argue that all of this is complete nonsense. Or, you can be smarter and use this "flaw" within the course to your advantage.

I spent a good year or so arguing with my grade-eleven TOK teacher that much of what we are taught is simply the IB's attempt to implement an element of philosophy into the syllabus. I would sit there and laugh at questions such as "How do we know?" and "What is knowledge?" – I honestly found it a joke. Then eleventh grade came to an end. My teacher gave me a C for the year and marked my controversial mock oral presentation a pathetic seven out of twenty. I had to learn from my mistakes.

The lesson here is that you are not doing anyone a favour when you try to deny what TOK is trying to teach – you suffer, your classmates suffer, and your teacher will get fed up with you as well. I know it sounds horrible, but it's one of life's most valuable skills – the ability to tell people what they want to hear. You need to understand that you are only in this course for a few years, so you might as well suck it up and try to get through TOK as successfully as you can – whether you believe the material or not. That is what truly separates the top TOK student from the bottom. It's not what you know, it's what others think you know.

Here's an example. For my TOK essay I chose a title about the boundaries between various Areas of Knowledge and whether they are permanent. Initially, I wanted to argue that the AoKs are somewhat superficial, and that there exist tens if not hundreds of other methods of classifying knowledge areas into categories. Basically I was arguing that the Areas of Knowledge that we learn about are not exactly *correct* – they are simply an "IB" classification. After having a talk with my TOK teacher, it became clear that this was not going to sit well with most examiners. While I could have potentially written a wonderfully creative essay about various interpretations of the Areas of Knowledge and what other intellectuals believe, I would not score very high. I needed to focus on what the TOK syllabus is talking about - I needed to write in their language.

This is hard to swallow, I know. I'm not happy that it's this way, but there is little you can do to change it. Your best bet would be to just play along and outsmart everyone else. Leave your controversial arguments at home and get ready to talk a lot of TOK lingo in your essay. This includes avoiding bias at all costs. Even if you think your country/religion/sex/race or whatever is truly the best in the world – avoid saying so and keep it professional. Your essay needs to constantly focus on knowledge issues, no matter how non-TOK the essay title may seem.

While on the subject of controversial statements, another common pitfall for TOK students writing the essay is to make generalizations. "Muslims do this," "Americans eat that," "Women want this," – avoid making these oversimplifications. You should know that no two people are alike, so don't make false statements about a group/nationality/country that have no real basis except your own stereotyping. This just reeks of an anti-TOK way of thinking and you don't want the examiner to know that you are that close-minded. You are going against the whole IB concept of making you an open-minded individual. Be very careful when using words such as "all," "mostly" and "usually." To be fair, you are more likely to write these statements by accident, which is fine, as long as you can spot and rephrase them before you send off your essay.

Examples

One of the factors that will separate your essay from other students doing the same essay will be your use of examples. Now, this being the IB, you need to make sure your examples are personal, unique and ethically correct. You need examples from other cultures and countries, and they need to appear researched and not just made up.

Now, one of the reasons I strongly suggest that you refrain from sleeping in your TOK class is because you might miss out on potentially good examples brought up by your classmates or teacher. Keep one eye open for anything that could be put into your essay. Go over your notes (if you bothered to make any) and remind yourself of some of the stuff that was discussed in class. Gather examples from newspapers, magazines, Internet or any other relevant source. You will need to filter this by throwing away the "poor" examples and carefully but rigorously summarizing the "good" examples.

Remember that you will be given credit in your essay for not only tying all the relevant ideas and arguments together, but also for drawing on your own life experiences and personal analysis. Make sure you throw in a few cultural and internationally diverse examples here and there. If you've lived in hundreds of different countries and speak ten languages, use that to your advantage. Include not only your own experience but also examples from other cultures with which you have become familiar. Your essay could end up in the hands of an examiner living anywhere from Poland to China. Use a wide variety of sources, but more importantly, make sure that they actually clearly portray the point that you are making. Avoid superficial examples that all high school students think of: Galileo, Francis Bacon's dictum, Inuit words for snow and embryonic research are worn-out examples – be original!

You will often be advised to find linkages in your IB subjects and you are encouraged to point out these connections. In the TOK essay this is also the case. If you are writing about something and then a little light bulb goes off in your head to tell you, "Hey, we actually discussed this in biology class," then make sure you mention that one way or another. You are likely to be reading great literary texts in your IB English class and learning about some of the most influential people in your history class, so why not see if there is any TOK-related stuff to talk about there.

As far as actual quotations go, I would not overestimate their importance. It's impressive to show the examiner that you appreciate what some of the greatest minds in the world have had to say about your topic, but another person's opinion is only worth so much. Use these more as a stylistic device, rather than as a method to prove a point. As a general rule, you can either start with a quote to set the mood or summarize with a quote to have a lasting and memorable impact on your reader.

As long as we are on the subject of examples, I would also warn you to avoid using examples which are not clearly connected to the topic in question. If you have included an example that you doubt has any real significant impact on the essay, then you're better off taking it out. Similarly, if you can't remember why you placed that example there, then it means it's not proving a point – take it out!

Marking Criteria

As with almost everything else that has assessment criteria in the IB program, the marking criteria is of the highest importance. Read the official IB instructions over and over again. Once you have come close to finishing your essay, sit down and pretend you are the examiner. Give yourself what you think you will get out of 40 points.

Do you have evidence to prove that you know enough about problems of knowledge and that you have experience as a "knower"? Have you included enough examples to illustrate your points? Have you answered the question as it is stated? Did you score 35+ points when you graded yourself against the assessment criteria? If you gave your essay to a fellow TOK student in your class, would he mark it +/- 35 points as well (something I recommend you do if you have helpful friends)?

Make sure you can answer yes to those questions. Pay extremely close attention to the descriptors for top marks in each category. Also, you should note that the first two categories give up to 10 potential marks (twice that of the other categories). For top marks in criteria A, Knowledge Issues, you must have "an excellent recognition and understanding of the problems of knowledge implied by the title" and your "development of ideas is consistently relevant to the prescribed title in particular, and to TOK in general." Does that sound like your essay? Can you get at least 7 or 8 points?

Take that type of approach for all of the different criteria. Some may be clearer than others. For example to score top marks under criteria D (Structure, Clarity and Logical Coherence), you need to have an essay that is "excellently structured, with a concise introduction, and a clear, logically coherent development of the arguments leading to an effective conclusion." So, even if you are a great essay writer and can structure your essay flawlessly, you might get all 5 marks in this category no matter how poor your TOK knowledge is.

Bibliography

Keep in mind that there is an actual grading criterion for your use of sourced material. In order to get all 5 marks in criterion F (Factual Accuracy and Reliability), you must have "an excellent level of factual accuracy, and sources that are reliable, consistently and correctly cited, according to a recognized convention." That is not asking too much of you. Make sure you cite all your work and use a well-known citation method to ensure your bibliography is 100% correct. Remember, even one mistake (such as misuse of quotation marks or italics in the bibliography listings) could cost you one or two marks.

I know it is perfectly feasible to write an entire TOK essay without consulting a single source. While I would normally tell you that this is OK – the fact that there is a specific grading criterion just for sourced material could spell trouble. Be on the safe side. Don't think, "Oh man, I don't have a single source, which means no bibliography, which means they have to give me all 5 marks, because there can't be any mistakes!" Unfortunately it doesn't work like that. There is still the possibility that you will lose marks for not having sources when you really should have. Do the wise thing and make the effort to include a proper bibliography. The IBO does warn that, "Essays which require facts to support the argument, but omit them, will be awarded zero." Don't take that risk.

Keep in mind this is not a research paper – the *Theory of Knowledge Guide* provided by the IB states that 'neither the [TOK] essay nor the presentation is primarily a research exercise'. Anything in excess of five sources for a 1600 word essay in TOK is a bit sketchy, because you are expected to rely on your own experiences and analysis more. Keep sources to a minimum but make sure you have something there. Please don't mess up and "accidently" forget to source an entire statement that you just ripped off from a newspaper article. You will probably get caught – and you will definitely feel dumb. That being said, if you don't bother to look up information, you take the risk of making statements that are clearly false. For example, if you can't exactly remember what year Columbus discovered America and write carelessly 1294 (instead of 1492) you risk losing a point or two for your lack of research (note: I highly recommend you DO NOT use that example). It's not a research paper, but if you do use specific sources, then please include a bibliography just as you would for the EE. All the works that you consulted, whether it be online, book, journal or television, should be included in the bibliography.

There is no guarantee that you will get 40 marks out of 40. My advice is to aim for right about there, and hopefully you will end up with 35+ points. If you follow the directions and marking criteria, there is absolutely no way that you should be getting anything less than 30. Make sure you get the easy points and try your best for the harder ones.

Presentation

Along with the compulsory externally-moderated TOK essay, every student in TOK must prepare an internally-moderated oral presentation which should last ten to fifteen minutes (for you, this means 14-15 minutes). There will also be a discussion period after you are done presenting. The TOK presentation is worth a total of 20 marks, which is half of what the essay is worth. In your presentation, you will need to be able to demonstrate an "understanding of knowledge at work" in a real world scenario. Although a presentation sounds like a fun and easy thing to do, there are many pitfalls that students come across. Hopefully the following guide will help you avoid them.

To be completely honest, I think it's unfair that an ambiguous and confusing task such as a TOK presentation falls into the hands of those who often tend to be inexperienced TOK teachers. How is someone, who is just as comfortable with the topic as you are, supposed to decide 40% of your final grade? Much of doing well on your presentation will, therefore, depend on you understanding how your teacher's assessment works and figuring out what interests them and how to use this to your advantage.

Alone or Together?

Simple. Alone. Look, take centre stage, take a deep breath and work independently instead of trusting someone else with your grades. Remember that if you work together, you will still be marked on your individual performance, rather than that of the group. So even if you chose Mr. TOK as your partner and stand around picking your nose while he dishes out grade A material for fifteen minutes, your personal grade will suffer.

By working together with someone else you will sometimes give off the impression that you didn't want to do the work yourself or that you felt working together would mean you would be required to talk less. The benefits of working with other students are group performances, added input of your partners, longer presentation – all of which means more depth and detail. The costs, however, are concerning. The focus will be off of you; if your partner screws up it will hurt your grade. Furthermore, you risk being overshadowed by your partner and most importantly the presentation loses its personal touch because it's no longer yours.

If you think that by working together you can handle larger topics more easily because you will have more than 20 minutes to present, then I suggest you change your presentation topic. Trying to be ambitious and handle large complicated and broad topics with two or three partners will only hurt your personal grade. It's absolutely fine to do a presentation by yourself as long as the topic isn't too general.

Chances are that the majority of students in your class will opt to work together. However, if you look at the "brighter" students, they will probably all be working independently. This is because they know that this way they are more likely to get an A. Don't take the added risk of working with someone else and take your presentation into your own hands.

Topic Choice

OK, tricky question. You are given the ultimate freedom when it comes to choosing your TOK oral presentation topic. There are absolutely no boundaries as to what you can do and how you do it. Given these boundless criteria, it is astonishing how many students fall into the trap of choosing aged topics such as "media bias," "stem-cell research," "euthanasia," "same-sex marriage" and basically anything that seems as if it's stuffed with TOK. Do not make this mistake. Nobody wants to hear ten different presentations on stem-cell research, no matter how "different" they are! Stay away from these traditional, yet troublesome topics. Not only is there too much to discuss, but you will also struggle to be able to fit TOK information into your presentation as well. I guarantee that more than half of your class will chose one of these more "popular" questions, but I also guarantee that you will score much higher if you choose something original and specific.

One of the reasons I strongly advise you to go to TOK class alert and not sleep through the whole hour is that you will miss out on valuable presentation/essay material. Whenever your TOK teacher brings up a news article or a story that he/she thinks is interesting for TOK, jot it down in big red ink. So much goes on in the world on a day-to-day basis that just smells of TOK material and yet you wouldn't normally associate with TOK.

For example, the TOK subject that I chose for my presentation was not particularly fascinating and did not fall into the cliché of TOK subjects done throughout the years. There was a news story that came out a few years back about how the state of Florida wanted to monitor the teaching of history classes in schools across the state. Potentially this meant that they could rewrite the textbooks and omit/exaggerate certain aspects of historical content. Also, this meant there was one ideal way to teach history – no ambiguity, no questions. Clearly this will send alarms ringing in the TOK headquarters – which is good news for your presentation, because you can spend a quarter of an hour explaining everything that is wrong. Other potentially good topics of interest could be "How can TOK be taught in strict Muslim countries without being biased?" or maybe even a presentation into how Wikipedia has changed what we believe to be knowledge.

The point I am trying to make is that you will be better off choosing a topic (preferably from the news) that deals a lot with controversy in knowledge and the problems of knowledge. The marking criterion specifically refers to a "contemporary issue." Remember that at the end of the day you will be making a presentation not just about your topic, but also about how your topic relates to the different Areas of Knowledge and Ways of Knowing. Do yourself a massive favour and find a topic that is original and that you know will be good to analyze from a TOK point of view.

The reason I knew about that Florida story was because my twelfth-grade TOK teacher (who was, hands down, the best TOK teacher I have ever seen) brought it up in a class. I immediately noted it down because I understood the relevance it had in the context of TOK. You need to do the same. No matter how bad your TOK teacher may be, chances are he/she is still doing some work. You spend two years with them, so they are bound to tell you something useful at least a few times during that period. If that still doesn't work, you will need to get yourself online and find a good story. Try to stay away from complex topics that will require a great deal of explanation but also avoid embryos/media bias/gays and so forth. Also, don't try anything too controversial and start showing pictures of dissected sexual organs or analyzing anti-Semitic Nazi propaganda in an inappropriate way. Shocking the audience and your teacher will not make your job of having a grade A presentation any easier.

Choosing something that is relatively specific, such as a news story, an article in a magazine or a scene from a movie is much more effective than picking something open-ended and vague such as the death penalty. This is probably the number one mistake that students make. They choose a topic that sounds appealing but is simply too broad and needs to be circumscribed. By choosing a topic that requires a lot of background knowledge and explanation you will forgo valuable time spent discussing the underlying knowledge issues. The most effective and high-scoring presentations deal with issues in which you wouldn't expect to find TOK aspects.

Method

You could make a poster. You could do a play-like performance with a few other friends. You could even do a high-tech PowerPoint presentation with smooth transitions and amazing special effects. Or, alternatively, you could grab a white-board marker and do a TOK presentation so simple and effective you will wonder why you didn't think of it yourself before.

Your critical analysis is what will get you the top grade for your presentation. From my experience, analysis is much more difficult to achieve when you have role play, or a staged interview, or even make a short film. Remember that you are assessing and evaluating the problems of knowledge and methods involved in answering the question "How do we know?" So if you can manage to do all of that in a ten-minute performance or movie, along with exploring your topic's general background – well, good luck to you.

The key to success in your presentation is making sure you touch on all of the necessary TOK terminology and explanations. From my experience, the best way to do this is also the simplest. Forget making complicated posters (nobody has telescopic vision anyway), or having an Oscar-winning performance. All you need is to ask your teacher if you can use their whiteboard for the presentation.

What you need to do now is to separate the whiteboard into three sections. This will enable you to separate your introduction (which should briefly explain the situation) from your main treatment of the TOK issues and your conclusion. Leave the middle section the biggest (half the board) as you will need to write most here. Make sure you plan all of this out a few days before your actual presentation by making an A4 paper version.

On the left side of the board you will need to provide a brief background and introduction to your subject. Remember that this should take no longer than two or three minutes. You can just bullet-point some of the main points of your subject or story. What happened, when it happened, and why it happened are all questions that should be addressed. Keep in mind that you will not be awarded marks for a narration of the key facts and information. Cover the facts quickly and filter out any facts that do not enhance your presentation. If you are still struggling to explain the facts and background to your presentation in less than three minutes, then a solution could be to distribute a handout summary to your audience beforehand.

The middle section of the board is where you will score almost all of your marks. This is the bulk, the core of your presentation. Remember that your presentation must investigate and critically examine the Ways of Knowing and Areas of Knowledge within the context of your topic. Along with that, you will need to develop and highlight all of the possible controversies (Problems of Knowledge) and pull it all off as if you know what you are talking about. This is not an easy task, I must admit. But it is exactly why this method that I am sharing with you is almost unbeatable. You will need to have the TOK diagram on hand.

Now, you need to take a good few days or so to think exactly which Areas of Knowledge and which Ways of Knowing are strongly connected to your topic and how you could analyze them. On the whiteboard, you will now need to draw a relatively large "spider web" and have segments branching out. For example, one branch could deal with "Perception as a way of knowing" in the context of your topic. Another could deal with "Natural Sciences as an Area of Knowledge," again strongly linked to your topic. By the end, you should have a good six to ten branches that deal with separate AoK/WoK within the context of your topic. The most successful TOK student can flawlessly make links between AoKs and WoKs when doing the presentation or writing the essay.

I must warn you, however, do not look for something that is simply not there. The only thing worse than lacking any TOK material in your presentation is filling it with obviously poor material that makes it clear to your assessor that you are just trying to touch on every AoK/WoK without actually having a worthwhile analysis. Don't think you need to include ALL of the Ways of Knowing and link each, one by one, to the Ways of Knowing and then link it all up to your topic – that would be just silly. Nonetheless, get this into your head: your presentation must focus on knowledge issues and not the content of your topic (which you briefly discuss in the introduction). Deliberate use of and linkages between WoKs and AoKs are instrumental in a successful presentation.

This part of the presentation planning is the most difficult as you will, perhaps for the first time throughout your TOK experience, actually need to really think about the TOK syllabus and material. I can't exactly give you any general hints and tips on what to look for because this varies largely from topic to topic. However, don't underestimate the power of your TOK books and materials. For example, if doing a presentation on the right to perform euthanasia, you could start by looking up "euthanasia" in the Appendix of your TOK books to see what they have had to say about it. So many students forget that the best place to find more material to include in their presentation is not the internet; it's the TOK-IB ready books.

I can bet that more than half of your class will do TOK presentations that go a little something like this: pick a cliché unoriginal social controversy, explain why, when and where, then give arguments for and arguments against. Oh, and then a cheesy uninspired conclusion. This approach has absolutely nothing to do with TOK. Presentations filled with an overview and description do not score highly – and the scores of your fellow classmates will reflect that.

You should be spending at least eight to ten minutes on this core section of your presentation. Make yourself seem interested and honest when running through each of the TOK branches on your web diagram. The key to impressing the teacher (your assessor) is to show that you know all the TOK mumbo-jumbo and what it means in the context of your presentation. Therefore, it is essential you pay close attention to how you speak and project your voice to your audience. I know that there are no specific marking criteria for your oratory and persuasive skills, but trust me – the more you seem like you know what you are talking about, the better your presentation will be.

The final few minutes of your presentation should be spent on the final third of your board/poster - the conclusion. This doesn't need to be groundbreaking, nor does it have it be completely open-ended. There are a few vital things that you must mention, such as a roundup of the problems of knowledge and your personal response to them. Before all of that, however, you may wish to just briefly sum up what your whole presentation was all about.

Your conclusion should be both evaluative and conclusive. Discuss any questions you still have, or other ideas that have come into your mind in relation to your topic. A clever way to round off the presentation is with the question, "why is all of this important to TOK?" You can even ask that rhetorically to your audience. Make sure your answer is well thought-out and shows personal involvement as well as a relation to other areas. For example, for my presentation, I concluded that the Florida law will not only have immense consequences for History classes in Florida, but we as Europeans should strongly value our "right" to be allowed to read and evaluate different interpretations of history. Make your conclusion valuable and engaging to your audience.

This is the part of the presentation where you can reconcile different points of view and explain your own personal opinion on the matter. Don't be afraid to express yourself, and even if you are leaning towards one conclusion, point out any possible bias or problems with your conclusion. Avoid the stereotypical "there are many points of view... none of which can be discounted... all of which have equal value," as this shows that you have failed to really analyze and think about the conclusion. Your conclusion needs to summarize what your presentation was about in a few sentences and also present some sort of a forward-looking view, perhaps the implication of your conclusion in the future. Make your final few statements the most powerful in your presentation.

Remember to plan your presentation out a few days before you are set to go. Have your whiteboard "plan" scaled down and drawn out on an A4 paper so that you know where each branch will be and what order to go in. You should probably bring along a few bullet-point note cards if your memory is not up to scratch. Don't fall into the trap of writing another TOK essay and simply reading it, sentence by sentence, to the class. This method of presentation will score very poor marks. A good presentation is never fully scripted, but is supported by a few keywords and note cards.

Have a few points jotted down, glance at them once in a while, but mainly keep your eyes on the classroom/teacher.

Speaking and Rehearsing

Although there are no specific points awarded for method or engagement of the audience, you should ensure that your diction and oratory skills are fully exercised. Avoid big vocabulary and try to speak in a clear and coherent manner. I can't teach you how to be a good speaker, but you can definitely improve yourself with practice. Stress the key words by speaking louder, placing emphasis on the end of your important sentences, and adding emotion where applicable. Also, make sure you don't rush your speech and become difficult to understand.

Engaging and involving your audience is a must if you want a successful presentation. If you notice your classmates taking a nap during your presentation this is certainly not a good sign – no matter how "dull" the TOK jargon and content may be. You will need to learn how to present boring material in an interesting manner (sounds impossible, doesn't it?). Don't lecture. Walk around the class, use hand gestures. Whatever you do, just don't keep your eyes permanently locked onto your teacher. Even if you are not personally involved and interested in the topic, at least make an effort to pretend you are!

Marking Criteria

Just as you would have done for your TOK essay, you will need to thoroughly digest the assessment criteria set by the IBO for the presentation. You will need to familiarize yourself with it. No matter how great and moving your presentation will be, if you ignore the essentials required in the marking criteria, then you risk losing out on vital points. My advice to you would be to find the marking criteria that will be used for your year of assessment (because they have slightly changed over the years) and print it a week or so before your final presentation.

You will need to be very honest when "grading yourself." Be a strict grader and run down each section of the criteria, giving yourself a truthful assessment as you go along. There are 20 points up for grabs, and you should be aiming for all 20, because chances are you will lose a point or two that you didn't expect when your teacher actually marks your presentation. There are four sections in the criteria, almost all of which deal strictly with TOK jargon. This is why it is so important that your presentation is packed with TOK analysis. There are no extra marks awarded for visual aids nor will you score higher for having an interesting or engaging presentation. Get this into your head: you do not need any visual props to make your presentation more interesting. You don't want to be labelled by your teacher as "yet another PowerPoint presentation." We are no longer living in the 90s; PowerPoint will not score you extra marks for innovation. This is the reason that you should stick to having a simpler presentation method (such as the one I suggested) and centre all of your discussion around TOK issues.

Criterion A for the presentation asks you to "identify a knowledge issue that is clearly relevant to the real-life situation under consideration." If that sounds too simple to be true then let me ask you why do so many candidates fail to ever say, "The knowledge issue at the heart of my presentation is..." and go on to explain the relevance of it? This is what I mean when I say that too many students simply ignore the marking criteria. Your TOK teacher is probably going to be holding a clipboard with the criteria paper and checking away as you do your presentation. You need to really digest the marking criteria and make sure you use key words from it to "signal" to your assessor that you are fully aware of the criteria and are aiming for top marks.

Some parts of the criteria are a bit more ambiguous and you will need to use your common sense if you want to get the top mark.

For example, criterion B, Treatment of Knowledge Issues, asks for the presentation to show "a good understanding of knowledge issues" in order to be worthy of the maximum 5 marks. Most of you will struggle to fully comprehend what is being asked of you here; however, if you follow my key steps in how to carry out your presentation, you should score fairly well in the Knowledge Issues and Knower's Perspective grades. Notice how nearly half of the marks available centre specifically around TOK issues, which backs up my point about making sure that most of your presentation is carried out with this in mind. You should be able to distinguish your strengths and weaknesses and then make an effort to improve on your weak spots.

I cannot stress this enough, but the marking criteria is once again of great importance. It's not as important as it was for the TOK essay (because it leaves a lot more room for imagination and is more vague); however, it still should serve as the basis for how you present. I'm not discouraging including interesting non-TOK discussions to make presentations livelier rather than a dull, TOK-based monologue, but do so at your own risk. You now know exactly what is required to get the top marks, so if you feel that you can do that as well as present in an original manner, then you can give it a try. By familiarizing yourself with the assessment criteria you will force yourself to focus on the knowledge issues at heart.

Presentation Documents

Filling in all of the presentation planning documents and presentation marking forms can be a boring task, but you should make sure that you put in maximum effort nonetheless. Remember that the only thing the IB will see from your presentation is the forms that you have filled out and your teacher's assessment of the presentation – this means that the forms are of great importance to you. Make sure that you describe the knowledge issues clearly and explain the aims of your presentation well enough for the IB to be able to understand. If, in the highly unlikely circumstance, your TOK teacher really screws you over and gives you a clearly biased and unfair grade, you may still have the chance to appeal – if you filled in your forms correctly and have a good case.

Referencing

As with the essay, the presentation is not intended to be a research exercise. However, you are 99% of the time going to require sourcing of some sort of factual information. To make sure that there are no questions raised over the reliability of your facts and figures, I highly suggest you make a bibliography of all the information you use. Do this on an A4 paper and do it in the same format as you would for your essay. After you're done with this simple task, print out as many copies as there are students in your class and distribute them before the start of your presentation. Oh, and don't forget a copy for your teacher!

That's pretty much it as far as the presentation is concerned. Remember that there is no general formula for having a grade-A presentation; however, if you follow most of my advice, I can almost guarantee that you will achieve 15 and above. Even if you choose your own unique presentation method but stick to the basic essentials provided in this guide, you will still have a high-quality presentation. Although the presentation is worth half as much as the essay, it's arguably more important because it is so much easier to score high marks. Your teacher will most likely be more generous than an IB examiner. Although I heard of many 20/20 presentations, I am yet to meet somebody who has scored above 38/40 on their essay. Just in case you somehow screwed up your essay, you might as well max out your marks on your presentation and pray for an A overall.

Teachers

There is no such thing as a TOK teacher. I am yet to see a school that hires a teacher to specifically teach TOK. Usually it is the English teacher, or the mathematics teacher, or some other poor soul who was kindly asked by the school to learn the TOK curriculum and teach it. I specifically remember one of my friends coming up to me and saying "This is ridiculous! He comes into class on the first day and you know what he says? 'I know just as much about Theory of Knowledge as you guys, so this will be a learning experience we will both engage in!" These may be familiar words for many of you, and it's nothing you should be too alarmed about.

Your TOK teacher does have specific responsibilities when it comes to your essay and presentation. For the essay, he/she should offer support, provide advice, ensure that plagiarism has not occurred and most importantly fill in the essay coversheet. You could consult your TOK teacher with regards to the essay title; however, they are not allowed to choose the title for you. It is also suggested that your TOK teacher goes over one draft before you submit your final copy, so ensure that your teacher doesn't forget about this.

You cannot hold your teacher accountable for being unable to fully teach the TOK syllabus. Chances are, they never really wanted to teach it in the first place. I would guess that about nine out of ten TOK teachers wish they didn't have to waste those hours every week. There are exceptions, of course. Those 10% of teachers who actually engage in the TOK course will truly open your eyes. Don't complain about your teacher just because he makes you guys watch "educational" movies every week on "TOK topics" and forces you to keep a "TOK journal" and makes you do other time-wasting work. There are thousands of other kids in your exact situation. Luckily for you, your TOK teacher doesn't need to be Mr. TOK in order for you to get your As. You do need to keep a healthy relationship as it is he/she who will be grading your presentation but that's pretty much it.

Resources

Certainly don't make the mistake of limiting your TOK research to this simple manual. There are some truly wonderful TOK websites out there. Some provide simple non-detailed hints and tips (like this book) whilst others actually focus on the TOK material. Make sure you spend a good weekend or two just bookmarking the sites you know you will need to refer to again. It's amazing how many former IB students have taken the time to post up their old notes and essays for the world to see. Be a good investigative TOK student and do some serious Googling for material that will help you write an excellent essay or complete an excellent presentation.

Some have even gone through the effort of making specific checklists for you to print out before you hand in your essay to make sure it's ready. Make sure to find some sample essays. Some have even been graded by actual TOK teachers – this will help you see where people make their mistakes. Reading a few will make a big difference.

As far as commercial resources are concerned, I can't really say much. In my school we had two different TOK books for anyone who was interested, so I never really bothered to see if there was anything better out there. Now, having a quick look around, I could find online at least six books authored specifically for the IB TOK class. My best advice for those of you who are interested in getting your hands on a TOK book would be to first contact your IB coordinator or TOK teacher to see if the school has a copy. If not, consult the IBO store and have a look at the TOK Course Companion that they offer. I don't know what it's like, but having read their Course Companion on other subjects, I doubt you will be disappointed.

Don't rush out to buy everything IB-related that you find on the Internet. Make sure you know that the author is experienced with the IB, and that the book is definitely TOK-based, not a philosophy book. Do explore what others have to offer, but at the end of the day, ask yourself whether you really need it or not.

What do I do in class?

At the end of the day you have to remember that it's not your weekly essays or mock presentations or class participation that will give you the three "extra points" for your IB Diploma – it's the assessment and assessment alone. This will be frowned upon by teachers, but it's the truth: you need to do the minimum amount to get by, focusing mainly on your essay and presentation. These are your priorities: 1 – the essay (worth 40 marks), 2 – the presentation (worth 20 marks) and 3 – your classwork/participation (worth nothing, really). This advice should not be stretched too far – you do need to take into account that your predicted grades are important. Your teachers could impose consequences on you if you lack respect for the class and most importantly you miss out on valuable essay/presentation material by sleeping through TOK.

Here's the bottom line: do the minimum amount of work in class to get by with passing grades and don't irritate your teacher. Start your essay and presentation as soon as you have enough information about it – don't force your teacher to tell you when to start. You don't need to be that "top" student who always answers the questions and hands all the work in on time.

You need to be the smarter student and do only what is asked of you: a grade-A essay, and a grade-A presentation.

Final Words

Well, there you have it: the definitive guide to obtaining top marks in your TOK and EE assignments. Perhaps the key lesson behind all of this is **efficiency**. The EE and TOK are only a pain in the ass if you make them that. Remember what is at stake – the chance to beef up your final score by three whole points.

Your performance on the EE and the TOK work will determine the number of diploma points awarded. Both are measured against published assessment criteria. It's really that simple.

Nobody is asking you to do the impossible when writing your EE, or to come up with amazing arguments in your TOK class. You are simply set one task and that is to get the top marks – no more, no less. If you have read this guide from beginning to end then, please don't let your efforts end here. Put this down and utilize some of the tips and hints found here and then come back for more consultation.

Lightning Source UK Ltd.
Milton Keynes UK

175658UK00007BA/10/P